From Marine to GOD'S MISSIONARY

The story of Bob Ries and Jesus Wept, International

Gotham Books

30 N Gould St.
Ste. 20820, Sheridan, WY 82801
https://gothambooksinc.com/

Phone: 1 (307) 464-7800

© 2025 *Robert Ries.* All rights reserved.

No part of this book may be reproduced, stored in a retrieval system, or transmitted by any means without the written permission of the author.

Published by Gotham Books (April 2, 2025)

ISBN: 979-8-3492-4057-7 (P)
ISBN: 979-8-3492-4058-4 (E)

Because of the dynamic nature of the Internet, any web addresses or links contained in this book may have changed since publication and may no longer be valid.

The views expressed in this work are solely those of the author and do not necessarily reflect the views of the publisher, and the publisher hereby disclaims any responsibility for them

TABLE OF CONTENTS

INTRODUCTION 1

CHAPTER 1 3
    SENSING GOD'S CALL 3

CHAPTER 2 5
    EARLY MINISTRY PREPARATIONS 5

CHAPTER 3 7
    GOING AND GROWING IN MEXICO 7

CHAPTER 4 10
    INVITATION TO SUDAN 10

CHAPTER 5 12
    CAN YOU HEAR THEM CALLING? 12

CHAPTER 6 31
    THE CALL OF THE NUBBA MOUNTAINS 31

CHAPTER 7 34
    NATIONAL ELECTIONS IN SOUTH SUDAN 34

CHAPTER 8 37
    ONE DOOR CLOSES AND ANOTHER OPENS 37

CHAPTER 9 40
    OPEN WOUNDS IN KENYA 40

CHAPTER 10 43
    TO THE CONGO AND BEYOND! 43

CONCLUSION 45

SOME FINAL THOUGHTS 46

INTRODUCTION

When I was a child, I spent endless hours playing with my little green toy soldiers and watching war movies. Many of those films had my childhood favorite actor, John Wayne who often portrayed a Marine. Even from my earliest days I always knew that I would go into the military so when I graduated from High School it wasn't any surprise to anyone when I enlisted and joined the Marine Corps.

I thought this was just a fulfillment of my childhood dreams and since I didn't know where my future was headed it seemed like as good a place to start as any. Little did I know then that this was part of God's perfect plan for my life. My wife Glenda and I spent 20 years in the Marine Corps and although she wasn't enlisted, she endured nonetheless through all the hardships that I had to bear. She was always faithful to be there and comfort me. Upon reflecting on those times, I admit there were hardships being a Marine, but to this very day I tell people that I actually enjoyed 90% of our time spent in the Marine Corps—and that is why I made it a career.

During that time, we attended church and I called myself a Christian, but at that time I did not have a personal saving relationship with Jesus Christ. After I retired from the Marine's we returned to our hometown of Millington, Tennessee having no idea what I would do. Over the course of the next two years I did a variety of things. Among those things was my first mission trip to the former Soviet state of Ukraine. Unbeknownst to me at the time God was working in me even at that time. I still called myself a Christian and Glenda and I were regularly going to church but more was going on behind the scenes of my life. God began to draw us towards the mission field.

The first real experience with missions for many people is through short-term mission trips. These are mission experiences which usually last for under two weeks. Many are one-week experiences. God first began to give us a desire about missions from that very first short-term mission trip to Ukraine.

It was also during this time that I began working for Federal Express in Memphis, Tennessee. I began work as a package handler in the Hub. It eventually led to a position as a Customer Service Trainer and what would be the best paying job of my entire life! I worked for Federal Express for just over five years. It was also at this same time that God continued working in our lives. We felt a specific and definite call to the mission field.

Glenda and I began planning on how we would go about entering full-time missions work. We devised a good plan, but in the end, God had a better one! Though I had a retirement through the military, God also provided a retirement for me from Federal Express even after only working for a little over five years.

How amazing is that? That retirement God provided has been a critical element in our ministry. When we are in East Africa (which today for our ministry includes South Sudan, Kenya, and Uganda and hopefully in the near future, the Congo) it would be impossible for us to do ministry without the finances from the retirements from both the Marine Corps and FedEx. While I have tried my very best to plan and prepare for the future for my family and I, the one thing that has made it possible for us to do ministry especially in Africa has been God's provisions and His perfect plan for our lives. It wasn't always clearly or easily seen, especially as we were living through it, but now as we look back, we see how God' hand providentially guided and provided for us in so many miraculous ways.

This entire book is nothing but our expression of our praises and thanksgivings to our Lord Jesus Christ who supplied our every need even when I didn't know what I wanted or needed. Wherever we go I first and foremost faithfully preach the gospel of Jesus Christ: that He is the Son of God, that He loved us and came to earth from heaven to die in our place, that He was buried and spent three days in the grave, that He rose the third day, afterwards that He ascended to heaven and now sits at the right hand of the Father awaiting His return to earth in glory. Beyond that I proclaim that Jesus is God in the flesh and that He has a perfect plan for each and every one of us. Furthermore, that if you will seek Him, listen to Him, and be obedient to Him, then His plan will always be better than your plan. This is what this book is about, God's perfect plan for your life. Amen!!!

"For I know the plans that I have for you," *declares the LORD*, "plans for welfare and not for calamity to give you a future and a hope. Then you will call upon Me and come and pray to Me, and I will listen to you. You will seek Me and find Me when you search for Me with all your heart." *Jeremiah 29:11-13.*

CHAPTER 1

Sensing God's Call

I had been retired for about two years when Pastor George A. Hern spoke about missions one Sunday evening at our home church, Crosspoint Baptist Church in Millington, Tennessee. Pastor George was a good friend of our own Pastor Scott. He talked about his mission work in the Ukraine and the many different things that he had experienced throughout his many years on the mission field. He had recently returned from a mission trip that he had made to the Ukraine where he made several good contacts. He was in the process of organizing another return trip in just a few months.

Until this time, I had never really seriously considered going on a mission trip outside the United States much less to a former Soviet Republic. However, by the end of that evening's service, all that had changed! Pastor George concluded the evening program with an open invitation for anyone interested in traveling and ministering in the Ukraine with him on this next mission trip to come to the front of the sanctuary at the end of the service and meet with him.

At the end of the service with his invitation extended, both Glenda and I jumped up out of our seats and literally ran to the front to join him in this mission trip! This was the beginning of our journey into missions. The trip was scheduled to last 10 days. As I think back on it, in reality it actually seemed more like a vacation than a mission trip. There were no real hardships, no suffering, and no back-wards cultural experiences. We had electricity and running water and were able to bathe regularly. Life was fairly good and so my preconceived ideas about mission trips radically changed. Some people go on missions' trips as more vacations than for spiritual reasons: to see places they've never see (and probably will never see any other way)! At one time I thought this was a misguided approach and I questioned their motives, but later I realized that even this was a tool for God's use to draw people into mission's ministry. That was the very way Glenda and I started our journey into missions.

Glenda was always well ahead of me in her devotion and commitment to the Lord. For her this was much more than just a mission's trip, it was a personal spiritual encounter with God. On the other hand, for me this was an experiment, a time to find out if God really could use me in His work. I soon discovered that He could use me if I would just make myself available to Him.

After this initial trip to the Ukraine both Glenda and I went on many other short-term mission trips. We went to towns and villages on the Mexico-United States border as well as other towns located in the interior of Mexico. Glenda went on with a mission's group without me to Cambodia in Southeast Asia. God was continuing to work out His perfect plan for our lives. He was in the process of drawing us to a permanent onsite mission's ministry.

It was during this time that I gained employment with the overnight shipping magnate Federal Express working as a package handler. After two years I moved to the corporate side of FedEx as a Customer Service Trainer. I look back on the five-plus years that I worked for FedEx as being very rewarding and enjoyable. When I worked in the Hub I would come home exhausted. When I worked as a Customer Service Trainer I was constantly learning new things; including ways to communicate with people. I now think how ironic that, after being in the Marine Corps for 20 years and working mostly with men, I was now a Customer Service Trainer working primarily with women, teaching them how to handle disgruntled and unhappy customers. Incidentally I had never been a Customer Service Representative before so I was teaching something that I really didn't have any experience in. I taught them how to use the computer system and how to treat people decently—even when they didn't treat you the same. You need to understand that when a customer calls FedEx repeatedly it's because a very important package didn't arrive on time. In some cases that can possibly mean thousands or tens of thousands of dollars in lost revenues. Under these circumstances it really doesn't matter why it did not either arrive or arrive on time, they're upset and unhappy that it didn't arrive when it was supposed to and want to argue and complain to someone at the company who injured them!

Once again, I can look back at and see that God was preparing me for what was to come. There is no doubt that my time in the Marine Corps represented a preparation time. Many times, when I talk to Christians about going to Africa they will undoubtedly say something like: "Oh I couldn't go there, there's no air conditioning" or "I couldn't possibly use an outhouse" or "I'm sure that I couldn't eat their kind of food." These are just excusing that some Christian's use so not to listen and obey God's call to go out to the world and proclaim the gospel of Jesus.

My time at FedEx taught me how to listen to people, try to understand and discern what their needs were, and how to best meet those needs. I can clearly see how my time in the Marines and the time at FedEx helped prepare me for God's calling to the mission field and all that it entails.

CHAPTER 2

Early Ministry Preparations

Not counting the short-term mission trips that Glenda and I made to the Ukraine and Mexico, the very earliest ministry experience we had was when I was preparing to leave Federal Express. Glenda and I had committed ourselves to full-time mission work on some mission "somewhere." We had devised a good plan: we planned to make triple mortgage payments on our house for three years and pay it off. We then would be in a financial position so that we could go to the mission field without any debt.

God honored that plan and went one step further. At that time FedEx was in the process of "downsizing" their operations. They were offering retirement incentives (buy-outs) for those who desired and qualified. The first qualification was that one had to have been employed with the company a minimum of five years. I had been employed with them for five years and five months. The second qualification was that one had to be a minimum of 50-years-old. I was 50 years and 6 months. I met the two qualifications!

This buy-out was going to pay me enough money to make my house payments every month. Even though I was technically retired already from the Marine Corp, I took the buy-out and retired a second time!

As part of the deal Federal Express also provided classes to help people prepare for their transition into retirement. Part of this preparation was regular meetings for retirees to attend. These meetings usually had anywhere from 40 or 50 people in attendance. The company provided all manner of information related to preparing you for retirement. One of the really neat features of these meetings was that everyone was given a five-minute time period to stand and tell the rest of the class what they were going to do in their retirement. I went to three of these classes. When my five minutes came, I would always share that my wife and I were going to the mission field and tell people about Jesus Christ. Our mission ministry actually started even before I ever left FedEx.

It was also during that time that I took several courses at the local Baptist seminary. While I didn't feel that God was calling me to obtain a degree in theology or missions, it just made sense to me to make the best use of the time available to prepare before heading off to the mission field. That time was time well spent. Dr. Steve Wilkes, one of the professors at the seminary, also did mission work in Brazil. I later made two trips to Brazil: one with him to the interior and one with his associate down the Amazon River. Sailing down the Amazon was a life-long dream! Just how good is God?

At the time I didn't realize that I would become a full-time missionary when I was going down the Amazon River. I had never really considered it a possibility. Glenda and I were going into mission work but were uncertain as to what that really meant. I believe that because of my obedience to Him that these mission trips were His reward. I got to travel down the Amazon, and God through His perfect plan made it possible. God just began to pour out His blessings!

Up until this time I had been in church and was doing all the "church" things for 30 years before Jesus became the Lord of my life. In times past, I had walked down the aisle at church and prayed the sinner's prayer, but somehow nothing seemed to have really changed in my life. Before the Lord called me to the mission field I had to have surgery inside my head. I was very concerned and once again I prayed to receive Christ—this time things were radically different! Immediately things in my life began to change in so many different ways. I felt the Lord calling us to full-time mission work, and we responded. After that, what so many people called "coincidences" began happening in our lives. The trip down the Amazon River was one of those, and through the course of this book I will mention many more things that I had no control over. Things just happened in spite of what I was doing and God was blessing in ways that I couldn't even begin to imagine.

CHAPTER 3

Going and Growing in Mexico

In March 2004 we packed all of our personal belongings and put most of them in the attic. I had talked to people at Mid-America Baptist Theological Seminary and had made arrangements for a student and his family to live in our house rent free while we were gone. They would be responsible for all of the normal maintenance duties and pay the utility bills as if it was their own home. I had just quit a job where I was making $75,000 a year and had no replacement for that money. Many friends and church members thought that we should rent out the house; that it would supplement our loss of income while living and ministering in Mexico. As reasonable as that sounded I didn't feel God leading us to do that. I felt him call us to make that house—His house—available to help build His kingdom. I felt that by making it available to a student who was financially struggling as he learned God's Word and prepared himself for a lifetime of service to Jesus Christ, that was a good use of the house.

We loaded the things that we needed into a pull-behind trailer and headed for Harlingen, Texas. At that time, I thought that these decisions were the most difficult decisions I had or would ever make. To out-right quit a job that had great pay, great benefits, and one that I enjoyed doing, didn't make any good sense according to the way the average man thinks!

During that time, I also spent an incredible amount of time in prayer seeking God's will. You may find God's will by praying, reading the Bible, and listening to the counsel of spiritually gifted people such as your pastor. At that time, I was certain that I heard Jesus tell me that I was going down the path he wanted me to go, but still it was very difficult for me to be obedient. I had spurious thoughts: "What if it wasn't Jesus talking—what if it was only my imagination?" "What if my thoughts were the result from something I had eaten the night before or what if it was the devil just wanting me to be a failure?" It was a very troubling time emotionally and spiritually.

We made the trip to Harlingen from Memphis in 24 hours. We pulled into town and had a place to stay at Way of the Cross ministries. The ministry had purchased an old hotel which had been condemned. The ministry was in the process of renovating it. We lived there for the next four years. We lived in an upstairs apartment of a two-story building. It had one bedroom, a bath, a tiny kitchen, and a living room. The electricity worked, well at least most of the time as did the air conditioner, but God provided for us very well.

How well I remember that we had just taken a $75,000 pay cut along with losing all the other benefits that went along with my job, but we never lacked for anything. God was so good.

The day after we arrived in Texas we had our first real introduction into mission's life. All of the rest of the missionaries living there were also part of it. It was a long orientation that I first thought was boring! After all, we had come down to do mission work and here I was sitting in an old room listening to the director of the ministry tell me things that I already knew—well at least I thought I already knew. As it turned out, I didn't quite know everything there was to know about missions and actually learned quite a bit in spite of my attitude and stubbornness.

Glenda and I began doing a variety of tasks around the ministry like everyone else. When I was in the Marine Corps my job changed regularly. Here at Way of the Cross Ministry you never knew when you went to bed in the evening what you might be doing the next day. I kind of liked that. It was a time for me to learn. It was an easy time because there was not a great deal of high expectations. I tell people that for the first six months that we were there that the two most time-consuming jobs I had were taking out the trash and transporting people in and out of Mexico.

I also had an independent and separate side job that was in support of Way of the Cross Ministry: taking photographs and making videos of the various church mission teams that would work with Way of the Cross ministries. Church mission teams would regularly come down to the ministry and cross the border and work in Mexico. I would try to go with every group at least one day. While there I would shoot pictures and, if possible, make video recordings. Then I would put a 10- or 15-minute video together of them doing ministry in Mexico. If they liked the video they could purchase it for a small fee. When the team left Way of the Cross and returned to their home church they would already possess a video presentation all ready to show. That was a primary job for about three years.

In that last year God was working on and in me. He took a person who was not interested in sharing his testimony or preaching the Word of God and began to grow those very desires within me. For that last year I tried to get with every group that came down to the ministry and share my personal testimony with them. (Your testimony, no matter how dramatic or mundane that it may seem, is the one of the most effective and powerful tools available for you to somebody about Jesus Christ!)

For a long time, Satan convinced me that I didn't really have a testimony. The reason he did that was because I actually have a very powerful testimony—I just didn't realize it at the time. You see I have been in church my whole life. I grew up in the Catholic Church and I spent about 20 years going to mass. I wasn't a very good Catholic; I was just an average Catholic going to church on Sunday and that was about it. When I met Glenda, her father said that if was going to date his daughter then I had to go to church—with them! They went to the Baptist church. At the time I didn't see much difference between Catholics and Baptists. Later we were married and so whenever we went to church, we would go to the Baptist Church. We did that for about 20 years. After I became a born-again Christian, I tell people that denomination doesn't make much difference to me. When I read the Bible, I don't see anything about Baptists, Pentecostals, or Catholics. The Bible and a personal relationship with Christ is what are supremely important.

When I was almost 50 years old I had a serious sinus problem that required surgery. There were two specialists that would be working inside my head at the same time. They said it wasn't anything unusual or special and that I shouldn't be worried about it. However, it was my head and I was worried about it. I also worried and wondered if I was truly born-again?

The day before my surgery I went to my pastor and sat down with him and told him of my concerns. He led me in the sinner's prayer. While I had prayed and said the words many times before, I believe this time was when I was truly converted to Christ. I was also at peace with the surgery. Not long after the surgery I first felt God calling us to the mission field and my life changed in many ways.

For the last year besides taking pictures and making videos, I was also sharing my testimony with all the groups and occasionally preaching very basic sermons. The Lord was doing a work in me. He was growing and preparing me for yet another great move. While all of this was happening, God opened a door for me to go to Nigeria, in western Africa. I had never previously had any interest before in going to Africa, but when this door opened, just as my first trip to the Ukraine, I jumped on it!

In Nigeria I found that God could use me as a preacher and a teacher. That excited me! While we were sitting in the airport for a 10-hour layover on our way back home, a pastor told me that he was going to go to Sudan in the next few months. He asked me if I was willing to come along with him. He said Sudan was much different than Nigeria; it was a much more dangerous place and that I shouldn't answer until I had seriously prayed about it.

CHAPTER 4

Invitation to Sudan

When we returned to Texas I began praying about the opportunity and invitation to Sudan. I also asked everyone I knew to pray along with me. My desire was to make the right decision and I needed their prayers as much as anything. The main question was: "Was its God's will for me to go to Sudan?" My great fear was to discern if this truly was God's perfect will for my life, or was this a case of me just wanting to go on an adventure to a new foreign land? If this truly was God's will for me to go I needed to know this absolutely and confidently and be obedient to His will.

By that time in my spiritual journey I had grown enough not to be looking for a vacation or an adventure, but I was still having a difficult time believing that God could actually use me, especially in a place like Sudan. Yet, if it really was His call, that I would be obedient to it. Proverbs 15:22 states: Without counsel, plans go awry, but in the multitude of counselors they are established. I believe the Scriptures are true, however if you ask a variety of different people what you should do you're likely to get a bunch of different answers—and I did!

Most people were very supportive of my going on this trip to Sudan, but I also had some that were not. There was one pastor who informed me that God definitely told him that I should not go! This really upset and bothered me. After all, this man was a pastor, and in my mind that meant he was certainly walking closer with the Lord than I. Consequently, over the next month while I was prayed I had that thought stuck in the back of my mind the whole time. I still had a difficult time believing that God could really use me in a meaningful way in Sudan. I was confused. I was seeking and listening for His word, and I wanted to be obedient, but how and why would the all-powerful Creator of the Universe want to use me in Sudan? Surely there were many other people that were much more qualified than me: people who spoke the language, people who knew the Bible much better than I, people who were greater prayer warriors than I. I know that if I were God I would use those people before I would ever consider me! The fact that this was a pastor really unsettled my already weak confidence!

I finally conferred with another pastor friend of mine. He took his Bible and turned to the passage in the Old Testament that talked about the young prophet and the old prophet. God gave the young prophet a task and told him exactly how to do it and what he could do and what he should not do. After he completed his task he was returning to his home. An old prophet met him on the way and asked him to stay at his house and have dinner with him. The young prophet replied and said "the Lord told me I could not stop, I should go straight home." The old prophet however told him that an angel had told him to stop the young prophet and to feed him. So, the young prophet stopped, had dinner, and spent the night with the old prophet. The very next morning after he saddled his donkey and was on his way home a lion appeared on the trail and killed him. The truth of the story was that you should be obedient to what God has called you to do and do not listen to others but stay with what the Lord has called you to do. God holds you accountable to follow His directions, not to do what somebody else has told you that God has told them. Upon this insight, I committed to go to Sudan with Pastor Oscar. This was the first of many trips that I would take to Sudan.

While we were there in Sudan I had the opportunity to share my personal testimony and meet many people. I needed to meet them in order to learn how to travel in that area. It was clear to me that this was God's way of opening the door for me to Sudan. This was my first trip to Sudan and I went with Pastor Oscar. He showed me everything I needed to learn to make many more trips in the future by myself.

Since that time, I have preached at many churches: I've preached at open air revivals, I've preached to the Army and to the police, I've preached in the prisons and the orphanages. Jesus Wept International ministries have financially contributed to help build schools and churches; we have provided materials to build bunk beds for the orphanages. JWI has donated computers and computer software for schools and also a wide variety of Christian literature to touch people's lives. These are just the material things; it doesn't count the hundreds of times that we preached the gospel. In both small and large groups, we have seen people come to know Jesus as Lord and Savior. There are times when we preach the gospel and no one responds to receive Christ. There are times when perhaps two or two hundred who respond to the gospel invitation.

On a couple of occasions, I preached the gospel to the Sudanese People's Liberation Army (SPLA) and saw over 150 soldiers pray to receive Christ. Some were from a Christian background; some were from a Muslim background, and others were from a tribal animist background.

CHAPTER 5

Can You Hear Them Calling?

Sometimes people will comment that Glenda and I are so dedicated, that we have so much faith, and how special we are for what we do both here in the United States, Mexico, and in Africa. My response to them is that we, like most Christians, are just regular ordinary people. It has been a long journey with the Lord, but I think the thing that has set us apart from others is this: we have made ourselves available for God to use us.

The Lord has been so good to us. He has grown us in our faith using very small steps beginning with our participation in short-term mission trips, something that any Christian can do. We saw that we could be used in ways that we had never considered. For a number of years, we made ourselves available to do various small term mission trips, yet we had an even greater desire to do more after participating in those trips. Consequently, for us the next natural step was to enter into full-time mission work.

One of the significant problems that we faced was that the major mission's sending organizations either didn't want us, or had requirements that were so overwhelming that it would take us years to be qualified. We felt God calling to missions—now, at this time, not years into the future.

When God led us to Way of the Cross ministries in Harlingen, Texas, it was an answer to our prayers and a way of making ourselves available to be used by God. If we hadn't listened to that call the opportunity to go to Nigeria may have never come and the invitation to go to Sudan most likely would never have materialized. I may have never discovered that Glenda and I could step out on our own and do ministry in East Africa. Once again let me say there is nothing special about Glenda and me. We simply make ourselves available to God to use. We live by what I teach in both Africa and the United States: seek Him, listen to Him, and obey Him.

Jesus has a perfect plan for each and every one of us. He has a plan for each person that's ever been or ever will be born. His plan will always be better than our plan and in order to discover what that plan is we have to seek Him. We do that through prayer, fasting, reading the Bible, and listening to godly committed Christians such as your pastor or other godly men and women.

The question many people ask me is: "How do you know when or if the Lord is speaking to you?" My answer is that He has never spoken to me in an audible voice, but the all-powerful Creator of the Universe could if he wanted to. Many times, He speaks simply to me through something I'm reading, He speaks to me through my pastor as he preaches and teaches God's Word, He speaks to me through the words of my wife and children, and He speaks to me through other people. God speaks, but I must listen for His voice.

One of the most amazing examples that I can give is of the Holy Spirit speaking to me is one day while I was preaching in a little village on the border between Uganda and the Congo. I had been there ministering for three days and this was the last day. I do not remember exactly what I was teaching about at the time, but in the middle of it I stopped. I turned around to get a bottle of water from off the table behind me, something that I frequently do. (When you're speaking for an hour at a time in the tropics you drink a lot of water!) I gave no thought to this action. When I turned back around with the 1.5 L bottle of water in my hand, I poured a little bit of water in the cap and explained: the water in the bottle cap represented everything that I had given them in the way of teaching from the Bible. The water that remained in the bottle was comparable to the knowledge that the Holy Spirit wanted to give them.

I was suddenly shocked within my spirit. I had never heard that illustration used before. I had never thought of that illustration. The only answer was that this illustration came from the Holy Spirit. That means that as I was speaking to the assembly, the Holy Spirit was speaking to me. You cannot imagine how amazed I was when that came out of my mouth! I say all the time that if we make ourselves available to Him, God will give us the very words that we need.

Can you hear Him calling you? You can if you seek Him, listen to Him, and obey Him. If you will do these three things then you may discern what the Lord's perfect and specific plan is for your life. He will guide you every step of the way. It is important that I say one other thing at this point:

1. Seek Him.

2. Listen to Him.

3. Obey Him,

And something just as important as the first three steps: Remember, God's will doesn't have to make sense to you.

If it had to make sense to me we would never have gone to Africa. To this day, even after having made the trip 10 times, it still doesn't make sense to me. I still believe that there are many more people who are more qualified than I, but I thank God that He has called me, that He has used me, and He has blessed me and my family in ways I could never imagine.

When I invite people to go with me to Africa sometimes they are concerned about the violence and danger. I tell them that the places I go are much less dangerous than the average downtown of any large city in the United States. Moreover, I really don't worry about the danger; I believe that there is no safer place to be than in the will of God. I know that that's where Glenda and I are.

When I speak to groups of people my ultimate desire is for them to share in the abundant blessings that God has poured out on us. It is so frustrating to me when I hear people make all the excuses that we used to make. We said that we didn't have the money, we're too old, what could we do, how could God use us? There's an excuse for every situation. Everybody can (and does) make excuses.

What God wants is our willing availability. I've never had the money upfront to go on mission trips, but that's never stopped us and I've gone over 10 times now. I like air conditioning and to be comfortable as much as anyone; I like electricity and don't especially like bugs, but those challenges are all minor in comparison to the bigger picture. In all the times I've been to Africa I have never been disappointed in how God used me or how He's provided for me.

In whatever God is calling you to do, listen to Him, trust in Him, and obey His word. He can and will use you. It will radically change your life for the better in ways you could never have imagined.

Crossing Equator, Uganda

Incomplete Hut at Macanke, Uganda, God's Garden.

New Baptist Out Post in Juba, Sudan.

In a canoe on Lake Victoria.

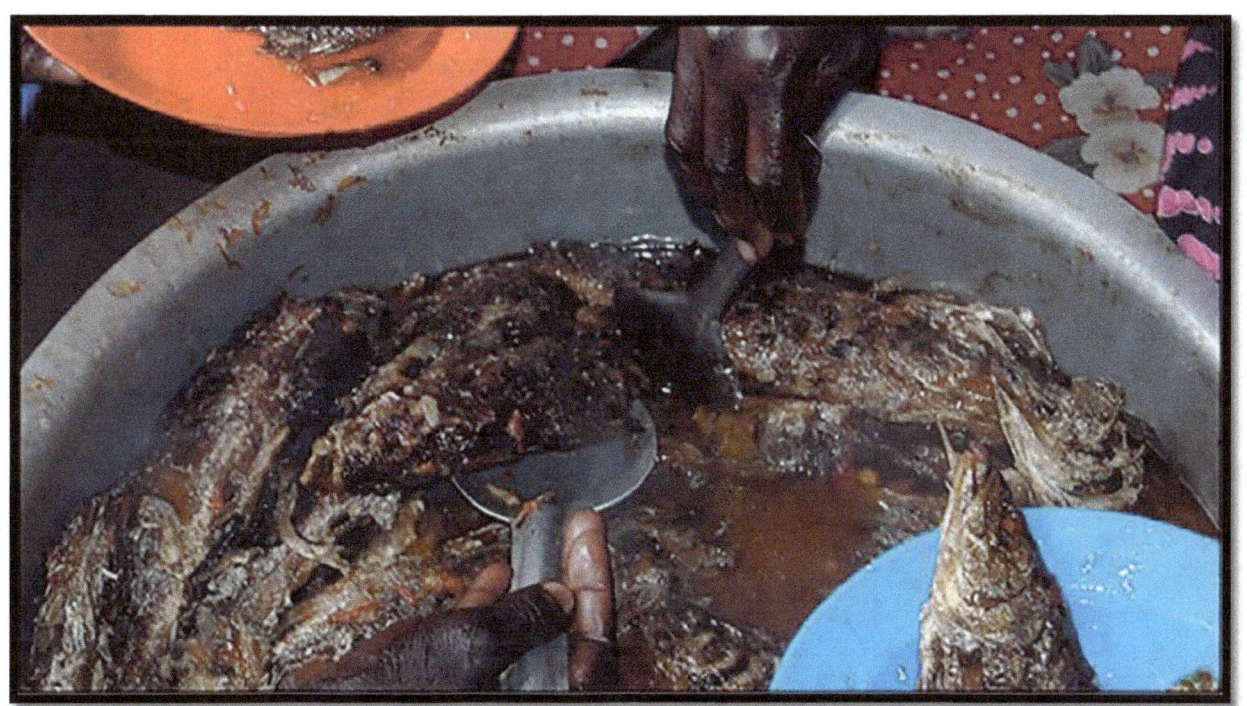

Fish for Dinner Anyone?

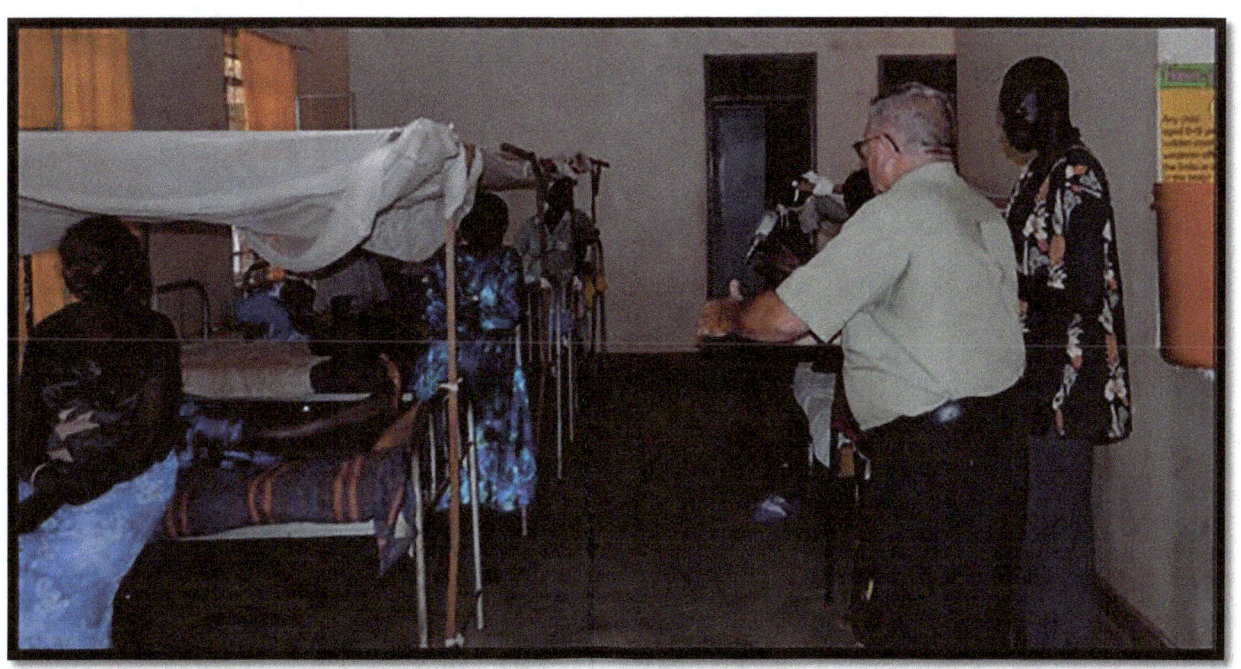

Praying for people in a Sudanese hospital.

SSGT Robert M. Ries USMC 1982

Economy Funeral in Uganda.

Robert Ries and members of SPLA (Sudanese Peoples Liberation Army)

Fishermen on Lake Victoria.

Presenting Pastor with Gospel Foot Ball

Sudanese Hospital (SAME)

Robert Ries with Pastors from Nuba Mountains in Sudan

Preaching in a school

Life in Sudan

After a day of preaching the Gospel.

My first Sudanese friends in Yei.

Catching a ride home at the end of the day.

Children taking care of children.

Masii Village in Kenya

Fishing Village on Lake Victoria

Children along a road in Uganda.

Children on Island in Lake Victoria 2012

Children in Village in Uganda 2013

Preaching Gospel to Army Base. Almost all accepted Jesus, including some Muslims. Two months later Civil War broke out and many of these men were killed including the Base Commander.

God had plans for me to speak at this school of over 400.
Most of the students professed to receive Christ.

These children collected termite larva to add to their stew for dinner.

Good Advice

Meeting People in the Mountains of Kenya.

Entering M i Hut in Kenya.

Distributing Bibles to SPLA in Sudan.

Preaching in mountains of Kenya to Massii.

Church members at small church in Uganda.

CHAPTER 6

The Call of the Nubba Mountains

Timing is important. Timing in missions work is crucial. On my first trip to Sudan I did not know exactly why I went when I did. At the time the calendar didn't seem too important to me especially since I really had no earthly idea what I was going to do when I got to Africa. After my first experience timing still wasn't too important to me. What was important was that I wanted and needed to get back to the mission field.

On my second trip to Sudan I began to see how timing was critical. I arrived on the mission site in the middle of the week. I contacted Pastor Stanley, the Director of Sudan for Christ Ministries. He informed me that because it was the middle of the week there were no church services scheduled. I spent the next three days not having anything to do except prayer walking around the mission compound. I was primarily praying for God to show me why I was there at that particular time since I felt that my time was being wasted no "doing ministry." Admittedly, I was a little aggravated with God. First, I had traveled all the way from the United States to Sudan to do mission work. I had arrived but there wasn't any mission work for me to do then. Second, I had prayed to God for the past three days and there was no answer from Him.

The very same day that I got aggravated at God, a lady whom I had never met entered the mission compound. She walked directly to where I was sitting and introduced herself as Rhonda Hall. She was a missionary with Across Ministries. They were having the 2007 Kush conference just one-half mile from where we were. There were people attending the conference that were literally from all over the world! The purpose of the conference was to assess the available resources and determine how they could best be used. Everyone attending the conference had to pay 100 U.S. dollars for room and board. I had a great desire to go but I was operating on very meager resources. Since I was an international visitor they invited me to attend and waived the cost. How awesome is that—for God to prepare me to attend an international conference that I knew nothing about, that was less than a mile from my very location, and furthermore, that He divinely provided the means by waiving the fee! This all took place while I was whining and complaining to the Lord about His inactivity to give me guidance and direction! He was answering my prayers and I didn't even know it!

The conference began the next day. The first conference speaker of the day was a pastor from a place in Sudan called the Nubba Mountains. There were actually three pastors from the Nubba Mountains in attendance but only the one pastor spoke. He spoke about a place that seemed to me to be the most primitive place on the face of the planet. It was a place where people were open to listen to the gospel of Jesus Christ. It was also a place where the Islamic government was bombing the predominantly Christian community, trying to run them off their land. He further related, "There are many missionaries here in the South, in Yei, but very few want to come up to the north where I live." Upon hearing that I heard a low-pitched voice speaking in my mind saying, "You could do this." At almost the same instant I heard another small voice say that there is no way that you could be useful in a place like that! Was that all in my imagination? Was that the Holy Spirit speaking to me or was it just my conscious expressing my human fears and doubts? Perhaps it was Satan? I really didn't know, but the seed of the Nubba Mountains was firmly planted in my heart.

The conference was a great experience and I learned a great deal from it. Not only did I gain new knowledge, information, and perspectives, I also learned a great deal from the events surrounding the conference. I was amazed that God brought me from half-way around the world to attend a conference that I knew nothing about, to talk to people about a place that I had never heard of, to direct my attention to a ministry that I was unaware of, and that He provided the means for me to attend.

I am absolutely convinced that God, in His perfect plan, guided me to that place at the right time which had nothing to do with my planning or preparation. Even if I had known about this conference I might have easily been too scared and intimidated that I would not have gone. I had to put into practice what I had taught so often to others: seek God, listen for His voice, and be obedient to follow Him. I had been seeking God for three days, I had been listening for His voice, it was now revealed. All that remained was whether I would be obedient to the heaven-sent invitation and opportunity. The question that I had to discern was: "Was this really God speaking to me?" To say the least I was very skeptical.

Over the next 30 days God showed Himself to me in a powerful way. It seemed that no matter where I went or turned somebody was telling me about this place called the Nubba Mountains. I went back to the Sudan for Christ facility. One of the young men staying there that I had known for two years, out of the clear blue sky, told me that he had been born in the Nubba Mountains and that his family was still there. The very next day I met a woman whose husband was a colonel in the SPLA and was stationed in the Nubba Mountains. A day or so later I was walking through the outlying bush, a place that I enjoyed and where I was very comfortable being off on my own. While I was walking along the path I happened upon a young man who spoke English. He said that it was very unusual to meet a white man walking through the bush. He asked me where I was from and I told him the United States—from the state of Tennessee. I asked him from where he was from. I was sure that he would say Yei, Sudan, but he didn't. He said that he was from, you guessed it! —the Nubba Mountains.

For 30 days I kept having those kinds of experiences. Wherever I was, either turning to the right hand or turning to the left, I repeatedly encountered people from the Nubba Mountains. The Nubba Mountains became an everyday reality to me.

When I left Sudan and returned to my home in Tennessee, I soon discovered to my amazement that there was a Baptist Sudanese church right there in Memphis! I contacted the pastor and told him I wanted to meet with him. When we met, the very first thing he told me was that he had been praying about planting a church in the Nubba Mountains, the place of his birth. I said to myself, "Okay Lord, I can take a hint; I know that you want me to go to the Nubba Mountains and I will be obedient."

This was no small commitment. Whatever resources that it took to travel from Memphis, Tennessee to Yei, Sudan, take at least that much more in resources to go from Yei, Sudan to the Nubba Mountains. From Yei to the Nubba Mountains is 1000 miles of dirt roads that have huge potholes something akin to the size of tank traps. You also must carry all your supplies that you need: water, gasoline, and food. You must travel in the dry season otherwise you will bog down in the mud. As a consequence of traveling in the dry season you may have to endure temperatures easily and often in excess of 100 degrees Fahrenheit during the day. This is not a place you choose lightly to go, but it was a place that I knew God had called me to go.

I have attempted to travel there for the past three years. I've gotten close twice and almost made it last year. My pastor friend from the Nubba Mountains had family members living in one of the many refugee camps located on the boarder. I had to make a hard decision. We could either drive our vehicle to the refugee camp and meet with and visit his family, or I could give the pastor the money for the trip so that he could take the bus and retrieve his family from the refugee camp back to the safety and security of Yei, South Sudan. I felt there was only one decision to make. Pastor retrieved his family. So, while I've been very close to going to the Nubba Mountains, I've never actually gotten there yet. Timing is crucial, but God's timing is always perfect and I know that I just have to be patient. He knows the day and the hour that I will get there and He also knows what I will do when I get there.

CHAPTER 7

National Elections in South Sudan

Just when I thought things were beginning to work out for me and the ministry in South Sudan, the government scheduled the national elections. Anyone familiar with Africa knows that it is never a good time to be in the country when elections are scheduled. There is much uncertainty in the air and tensions among the people can easily spill over into violence.

In my promotion and publicity of the ministry I had invited hundreds of people to come with me to Africa. From those hundreds of appeals, I finally had two people respond to return with me and actually put up the money to go. I was elated! I called Pastor Stanley in Africa to make final arrangements. When I called he said that God told him that I shouldn't come because the chances of violence and danger were too great. I responded that I also had been praying about the situation but that God had not told me not to go. Pastor Stanley responded tersely and informed me that should we come to Sudan; he would not have anything to do with us and that we would be completely on our own! I continued to plan and prepare to return and bring these two pastors with me anyway.

Personally, I was pretty comfortable in South Sudan but not so comfortable that I was willing to take other people with me without having proper or adequate support there. Once again, I was distraught and very confused. After years of inviting people to come with me to minister in Africa, I finally had not just one, but two who were willing and able to travel with me! I wasn't sure we had a place to go. I began to wonder: "Did I miss what God was telling me? Did God really tell Pastor Stanley I shouldn't come? How could God be telling me one thing and pastor Stanley something else?"

What a conflict! In my mind, one of us had to be right and one of us had to be wrong; it couldn't be both ways, or could it? I continued to pray and seek God's face. After a couple of days, I recalled a man that I had met in Memphis several years previous who ran a Bible school in Jinja, Uganda.

The airplane tickets that we had already purchased got us as far as the infamous Entebbe airport in Uganda. It was only a short drive from there to Jinja. I called John and reintroduced myself to him. I related to him the situation we faced with Pastor Stanley. I asked him that if we came to Jinja did he believe that we could do ministry in that area? He said that there were plenty of ministry opportunities and furthermore, he had a pastor friend who had graduated from Bible school and was just the man to guide and take care of us. That is when God brought Pastor Frederick into our lives.

This is one of dozens of times where God was doing something that was totally beyond my understanding. When I think back to those events I now realize what a tremendous miracle it was from Him. If Pastor Stanley had let us come to Sudan I would've never met Pastor Frederick. Up to this point we had only done a small amount of mission work in Uganda. If I had just said that God had called me to work exclusively in Sudan and that if I can't work there I just won't go, then I would never had met Pastor Frederick and missed one of the biggest and best blessings in the ministry.

Pastor Stanley told me that God told him I wasn't supposed to come there. I now believe that was absolutely true—even though I thought he was over reacting and being stubborn! At the very same time God had not told me that I wasn't supposed to go to Africa. We had already made plans and bought airplane tickets. I was once again naturally confused. I went to prayer and recalled to memory the man that I had met years ago. I contacted him and a completely new door opened up. There's a song that says God will make a way where there is no way. That is so true. We just have to seek Him, listen to Him and be obedient to Him.

Americans want to understand everything that is going on. We want to know all the details and how all the little pieces fit together in the plan. Things are supposed to be logical and make sense to us. I cannot tell you how many times people have told me: "God wouldn't do that, it doesn't make any sense." Why would we think that the all-powerful Creator of the Universe, the One who spoke the words and the universe came into existence—why would we think that the way He works would make sense to us? The difference between mankind and Jesus Christ is like the difference between a cockroach and a human being.

Jesus Wept International has been working with Pastor Frederick for over three years now. We have a very strong partnership and I trust him with my life! We still continue to work in Sudan and the ministry is growing there, but during these last three years we have expanded our work in Uganda and have branched out to working in Kenya as well. The ministry is growing. We've been all over Uganda including a very unique ministry among the fishing villages on some of the islands in Lake Victoria. The fishing villages on Lake Victoria are very primitive and most of the mainland pastors don't even travel there. Not many of the islands have churches and so the ministry is fruitful and wide open.

Last year we also worked on the borders between Uganda and the Congo. There were many pastors from the Congo that attended our pastor's conference. They also invited us to come to their country and visit their villages. They would gather groups of pastors from around the region and we could preach the gospel and train their pastors in how to reach the people in their areas.

This brings up another area that amazes me. For the past two years we have conducted pastor's conferences in Sudan, Uganda and Kenya. Here is the amazing thing—I've never been a pastor and yet we're holding pastor's conferences! God has an unusual sense of humor! That doesn't make sense to me but God has opened that door for us to walk through. What I teach is 99% taken directly from the Bible. Occasionally I may personally expound on what the Bible says about a particular subject, but when I do, I make certain that everyone understands that this is my opinion—what I believe. I may go beyond what the Bible clearly says but it is a clear interpretation of what the Bible teaches.

CHAPTER 8

One Door Closes and another Opens

What I had originally thought was an absolute disaster turned out to be perhaps the greatest blessing that the Lord ever bestowed on the Jesus Wept International ministry! Though I couldn't see it at the time I just had to have faith and work through it all. I believe that I did much more praying during that time than I'd ever prayed before.

When I talked to John the director of the Bible school in Jinja, and he told me that he knew a man whom he had great faith in that would work with us, I felt like I was out of the woods. I didn't know how it would work out, but what had started out to be an absolute disaster I felt was going to be a good opportunity to do the Lord's work. Little did I know then just how effective that Pastor Frederick and Jesus Wept ministries would become. (Not that there was anything special about me but because we had all made ourselves available for the Lord to use in whatever way He would. He showed us again, both that His plan is always better than our plan and that He would use us if we simply made ourselves available to Him.)

The first two weeks of the three months that I worked with Pastor Frederick was time dedicated to doing ministry with the two pastors that had come along with Glenda and I. When they left and returned home things in Africa really got interesting!

One of the first things Pastor Frederick told me was that he had some contacts in Kenya and thought that we should go there and minister to them. While I had not considered going to Kenya, I also told him that God hadn't said anything to me about going to Kenya. However, I did tell Pastor Frederick that I would pray about it, which I did. After some time in prayer, I felt a divine compulsion that we should indeed travel to Kenya. (Remember, God sometimes speaks through other people.)

We went to Kenya and stayed there a week. For the week that we were in Kenya we spoke at a variety of different places: churches, schools, and individual homes. We saw many people come to know Jesus as Lord and Savior and we also lifted up the local body of believers.

I didn't quite understand the pastors that we worked with. They were very devoted both to their people and to the Lord. I've heard Pastor Frederick speak and he preaches far better than I, but it means so much to the churches when a visitor from across the ocean so many thousands of miles away takes the time and makes the effort to worship with them, they wanted to hear me preach and tell them about the love of Jesus Christ. It just amazed me beyond words that the Lord could use me (or anyone who makes themselves available to Him) to encourage the body of Christ. That's why I always invite people to travel and minister with us. All they have to do is encourage people and show them the love of Jesus Christ. It will change the lives of the people to whom we minister and just as importantly, it will change the lives of the people doing the ministry.

It wasn't very long after we returned to Uganda from Kenya that Pastor Frederick once again came to me and said he knew of some pastors that had small churches located on small islands located on Lake Victoria. These were fishing villages where anyone rarely goes to minister. He said the Lord told him that we're supposed to go out and minister to the people in the fishing villages out on Lake Victoria. I responded once again and said that the Lord hadn't told me anything of the kind! I had never considered going out on a lake the size of Lake Huron in a canoe! I did tell him that I would once again pray about it. As I prayed I once again felt the presence of the Lord and Him revealing to me that we should indeed go and minister to the fishing villages out on the lake.

This made me very nervous. I can swim but I can walk a lot farther than I can swim. Besides, I've never swam in a lake that had crocodiles! To be fair, I've never seen a crocodile while in Africa but I have done the research and National Geographic as well as other people in the area tells me there are crocodiles and hippos in the lake. (Unbelievably, more people are killed in a year by hippos than crocodiles.)

We made our plans to visit three fishing villages over three days' time. We got in the oversized canoe and rode four hours out on the lake. At one point I couldn't see land anywhere. Even though it was a calm day the waves were still about 5 feet high.

When we stopped at the first island it was as if the whole island came down to see us! There were many people on this island that had been born and had never been off the island much less to the mainland. Many of the young people had never ever seen a white person before either. At first, they just stared at me and some followed me wherever I went on the island. Eventually the younger children adjusted to my looks and trusted that I wouldn't harm them. They would come up and rub the hair on my arms. They would look at my hands to see if the color would rub off on them.

When we had our church service we had many adults in attendance but all the children gathered around the outside of the main building we were in. Sometimes they would look in through the doors and other times they would just stand around outside. If I came outside they would run away but in the course of the day we spent a lot of time talking to those children and many of them learned about Jesus Christ. Some of them also learned that there were white people in the world who wouldn't necessarily harm them.

We left for the second island as the sun was going down and we arrived just before dusk. I could see that there were millions and perhaps billions of small bugs in the air that looked to me like mosquitoes. It was my worst nightmare! I could just imagine how these mosquitoes would attack and bother us. It was going to be a very long 24 hours! We eventually had to drive through this huge cloud of bugs, but instead of mosquitoes they turned out to be what they called lake flies. Although they were an annoyance when they were all around you and if you took a deep breath you could swallow hundreds of them, yet they didn't bite. So, one of my worst fears never materialized. I have found that's the way it is most of the time, the things that I fear the most never happen. (Fear knocked at the door, faith answered, there was no one there.)

The ministry on that island was beyond words. The people were so kind and loving. The Lord moved in a mighty and powerful way so that people came to know Jesus as Lord and Savior. After 10 years it still amazes me, I don't understand why God would choose to use a sinner saved by grace like me! But He did and I'm glad of it!

When the entire three-month mission trip was ended and I returned to my home in Millington, someone asked me, "What was the best part of the three months you spent in Africa?" I reflected on the question and finally told them about those three incredible days on Lake Victoria ministering in fishing villages at one of the most remote places in Africa. It was one of the most fulfilling and rewarding experiences of all times.

I had to really struggle at first to go out to those fishing villages. My flesh was saying that this is way above and beyond the call of duty. If other missionaries and local pastors don't go, then why should we? The answer of course was because God had called us to go there. He shared the need with Pastor Frederick and Pastor Frederick shared the need with me. Consequently, I sought God; He spoke to me and told me that He wanted us to go. I had sought His will, listened for His voice, and now it was time to obeyed Him. We did and He blessed me more than you could ever imagine.

CHAPTER 9

Open Wounds in Kenya

We have been going to Kenya now for three years. The amount of time we spend there each year has increased as well as the geographic area that we cover. On this last trip the Lord blessed us in an incredible way. First, He opened the door for us to go to southern Kenya and preach to the Masai tribes. The Masai are unusually tall, often attaining heights of over seven feet. They are also considered one of the fiercest warrior tribes in all of the African continent. Another incredible blessing was that it seemed like everywhere that we went to preach the Word of God we encountered those "wild" animals normally associated with Africa e.g. elephants, hippos, baboons, lions, gazelles, etc. Sometimes we encountered them in animal preserves and sometimes even along the road.

I've always been interested in animal programs on television and I naturally desired to see "wild" animals in their natural habitat. However, for the first seven or eight years that we've been traipsing all across Uganda, Sudan, and Kenya, we have never seen any wild animals! The only animals that we encountered were dogs, cats, goats, chickens and some ducks! So, it was a tremendous blessing to be able to finally drive around not one but two different nature parks and see all these various wild animals. I considered this to be a tremendous blessing of God. (When I would come home people would always ask me what kind of animals I saw. I found it disturbing that these Christians were more interested in the animals that I saw than about the people to whom I'd been sent to preach the Word of God.)

An even greater blessing than seeing these animals was the opportunity to preach and get to know the Masai people. We had set aside one day just to visit the nature parks. Though we were in the area we still had to drive 50 miles over very bad dirt roads. Just as we were starting to go into the park we had to driving down the side of a mountain. Located on the right was a Masai village. We made a mental note that on our way out we needed to stop and talk with them.

When we entered the park the very first thing we saw was elephants and a variety of Gazelles. As we continued through the park we saw lions and cheetahs. Later we encountered hippos, water buffaloes and giraffes. These were just a few of the animals we saw. The pastors also enjoyed themselves and this was a tremendous blessing to me.

As we left the nature park we labored back up the side of the mountain road which we had earlier descended. The road can only best be described as a narrow lane where water had just run down and washed the dirt away leaving only a rocky path. We finally arrived at the Masai village.

Their Chief came out, greeted and began to talk with us. We told him who and what we were—missionaries coming to preach the Word of God about Jesus. He was not impressed. He told us that we could walk around, meet and talk to the people but it would cost us 500 Kenyan shillings! 500 shillings converted to United States currency was equivalent to about six dollars. We paid the fee and began to walk and talk to the people. We also distributed Scripture coins.

These Scripture coins were about the size of an old American silver dollar and made from highly polished aluminum. The Scriptures were engraved on both sides in the Masai language. On one side was John 3:16, and other verses on the reverse side. There was a small hole drilled through the top of the coin so that you could run a string or small chain through and wear it as a necklace. We gave one to everyone in the village, from the youngest baby to the oldest adult.

That was the most amazing thing that I think that happened to me on that whole trip. You need to realize just how primitive this village was. The huts that these people live in are made the same way they have for hundreds of years. When you enter you must bend over at the door because the doorway is so small. It is only way in or out. There are no windows so the inside is always dark and damp.

As we were preparing to leave the chief spoke to us through an interpreter. He told us that if we would give him advance notice next time that he could arrange for other similar villages to gather so that we could tell them about our Jesus. He then did something that totally shattered all of my perceptions of his culture and existence. He reached inside of his traditional Masai dress robe and took out a cell phone! He then asked for our contact number and gave us his number.

I was totally dumbfounded. Here we were in the middle of Africa, in the middle of the most primitive village that I've ever seen, a village that had no electricity, and then for the Chief to pull out a cell phone was beyond belief. Africa is such an amazing place and the Lord works in mysterious ways.

We had made arrangements for the next day to visit with another Masia Chief in the area where we were staying. Our contact person in this area knew him and had made the arrangements for us to conduct church services in his village. We were told that it was very close to where we were staying and would only take a few minutes to drive there. It was true that it only took a few minutes to drive to the bottom of the mountain, but they had failed to mention that we had to walk up the side of the mountain in order to minister to this village! We had to stop three times to rest while going up the mountain. By the time we got there everyone in our team were so weary and worn we all thought we were going to die—Africans and Americans alike!

I was sweating profusely and was weakened by the trek. Besides needing to lie down to rest, I had also developed stomach and intestinal issues. As we rested the people continued to arrive. The service began. After a short greeting it was my turn to preach. In my depleted condition the only thing that saved me was that before I began to preach they had a short ceremony where they presented gifts to me. They gave me a traditional Masia robe and an authentic Masai gourd for carrying goat's milk, and from the looks of it you could tell that if had been fully tested!

The village had a small Christian church building and this is where I spoke. They also made me an honorary elder of the congregation. After all of those proceedings I felt reinvigorated and reenergized to preach the Word of God to them in one of the most beautiful places that I have ever been. God is so very good!

CHAPTER 10

To the Congo and Beyond!

During our last trip to East Africa we were on the border between Uganda and the Congo conducting one of our pastor's conferences. We were way back in the mountains deep in the bush. It is typical to have pastors travel from about a 50-mile radius. Some of the pastors at this particular conference were from the Congo. As it happened, these wanted us to come to their country and church upon our next visit. Currently that is just not possible at this time.

What we really want to do is choose one or two pastors in an area at least 50 miles from where we're at and have a service in their church. Our policy is to attempt to return the next year to the original church that we first attended in that area. We're attempting to build long-term lasting relationships with the pastor and not just conduct services where we can get the biggest numbers.

I believe that this is the best means to reach out to more and more pastors, their congregations and the lost people in those areas. The problem (if you can really call this a problem) is that our ministry is doubling or even tripling in size each year, but our resources to meet those needs are not keeping pace with the expanded ministry. Our Lord Jesus Christ continues to bless us in virtually every way imaginable, but I must confess that I get very impatient at times.

I'm waiting for more people to partner with the ministry both with their participation to travel to Africa with Glenda and I or partners who will stand with us financially and assist the work in that fashion. I long for the day when I plan out the budget for a mission trip is actually fulfilled and fully funded. It might seem like I'm complaining and I admit that I'm struggling with these issues, but there is such a tremendous opportunity here: people are so eager and hungry to hear God's Word. It breaks my heart knowing that on each trip that I take that I may meet people who will have died by the time I return to the same area. Many times, they die of such things like malaria, dysentery, cholera, and, believe it or not—traffic accidents! Many things that are easily treated in the United States are considered life-threatening in Africa.

It's sad to say, that the average American Christian has very little interest in missions. Instead of the church in America reaching out to the world, it has turned its focus and attention inward. Many pastors are primarily interested in their flock and church alone. Now I realize that the pastor of the local church has a responsibility to the members of that church but he has an equal or even greater responsibility to follow Jesus and obey His command to reach out to the lost and dying world.

There is not a day that goes by that I don't wonder why Jesus chose Glenda and I for this ministry. I wonder that if he had chosen someone else he might be better at motivating and inspiring people to get involved in missions and ministry. He might be better at raising the funds necessary to do God's ministry. I know that he would be a much better preacher of the Word.

I also know that perhaps with God's grace and provisions we can this coming year (2015) reach out and enter the Congo. And who knows what else is in God's perfect plan for us—maybe, just maybe you are supposed to go with us?

CONCLUSION

I didn't want to write this booklet. I am neither a writer nor an eloquent speaker. Many times, I struggle with the English language, yet at the same time I felt the Lord compelling me to write this. I really just wanted to argue with Him about it. So, what is the purpose of this book?

I believe that when people read this they will see how unprepared Glenda and I were for doing ministry; whether in Mexico or Africa. Yet they will also understand that God has a perfect plan for all of us just as He has for me. His perfect plan is available to you if you're willing to make yourself available to Him to be used in His service. He will use you!

Of all the things that you don't know how to do and all the reasons (excuses) that you make for why you can't serve, really demonstrate just how powerful Jesus could be in your life. The Bible says "I can do all things through Jesus Christ who gives me strength" (Philippians 4:13). If you've called yourself a Christian for any length of time, you've more than likely heard that verse. Christians often quote it glibly and then turn right around and exclaim what they can't do! That doesn't make any sense!

If we believe that Jesus Christ really is in control and that He indeed has a perfect plan for your life then you need to show it by trusting God and stepping out in obedience and in faith. We need to seek Him, listen to Him and be obedient. He doesn't make mistakes—He never has and never will!

He's known you even before you were in your mother's womb. He loves you more than you can ever imagine or understand. I implore you in the name of Jesus to just make yourself available to Him.

That is the message and purpose of this book. It is something that I am sure that you are probably very familiar with even if you don't want to acknowledge it. God is working in you. The real question that you must answer is: "Will I respond to God's voice? Will I seek Him, listen for His voice, and will I obey His call?" My prayer is that you heed His call. God bless you!

SOME FINAL THOUGHTS

The most significant action that you can take is for you to read and re-read this book while praying and considering its message. This book should not have cost you anything. The full price has been covered by Jesus Wept, International. I ask that you might begin to regularly pray for Glenda and I and the ministry of **JWI.**

If you feel the Lord calling you to do more, then please contact me. We always need workers for the harvest. And while the gift of salvation is free, the ministry of sharing the Gospel is not. JWI is always in need of financial support.

My prayer for you is the Jesus would bless you as much as He has us.

Robert M Ries, Director of Jesus Wept, International

4342 Bennett Wood Dr., Millington, TN 38053

You can email us at: rries52@msn.com/

or call us by phone: (901) 508-2000

www.ingramcontent.com/pod-product-compliance
Lightning Source LLC
LaVergne TN
LVHW081509060526
838201LV00056BA/3019